Music Math Workbook: Volume 1 encompasses mathematical equations and musical notation to help music and general education students alike with practicing the manipulation of musical note and rest values, and practicing simple math equations.

These equations can be given as homework and also be used in the classroom in fun group settings.

This book is dedicated to the members and supporters of Gwinnett Academy of Music. Thank you for your continued support and dedication.

Music Math

- **Addition**

- **Subtraction**

- **Multiplication**

- **Division**

- **Exponents**

- **Radicals (Square Roots)**

- **Algebra**

- **Combination**

ADDITION

1. 𝅝 + 𝅗𝅥 =

2. 𝅝 + 𝅝 =

3. 𝅗𝅥 + 𝅘𝅥 =

4. 𝅘𝅥 + 𝅘𝅥𝅮𝅘𝅥𝅮 =

5. 𝅗𝅥. + 𝅗𝅥 =

6. 𝅘𝅥𝅮𝅘𝅥𝅮 + 𝅝 =

7. 𝅝 + 𝅗𝅥 =

8. 𝅘𝅥 + 𝅝 =

9. 𝅘𝅥𝅮𝅘𝅥𝅮𝅘𝅥𝅮 + 𝅗𝅥. =

10. 𝅘𝅥 + 𝅘𝅥𝅮𝅘𝅥𝅮𝅘𝅥𝅮 =

11. ♫ + ♫ =

12. 𝅘𝅥𝅭 + ♪ =

13. 𝅗𝅥𝅭 + ♬ =

14. 𝅝 + 𝅗𝅥𝅭 =

15. ♪♫ + ♪ =

16. 𝅝 + 𝅗𝅥𝅭 + 𝅗𝅥 =

17. 𝅘𝅥𝅭 + 𝅗𝅥 + ♪ =

18. ♪ + 𝅗𝅥𝅭 + 𝅝 =

19. ♫ + ♬ + 𝅗𝅥𝅭 =

20. 𝅗𝅥 + ♫ + ♪ =

21. 𝅝 + ♬ + 𝅗𝅥 =

22. 𝅗𝅥 + ♬♬ + ♪ =

23. 𝅗𝅥 + ♪. ♪ + ♪ =

24. 𝅗𝅥. + ♩ + ♫ =

25. ♫ + 𝅗𝅥. + 𝅝 =

26. 𝅗𝅥 + 𝅝 + ♪ =

27. 𝅝 + 𝅗𝅥. =

28. 𝅗𝅥 + 𝅗𝅥 + 𝅗𝅥. + ♫ + ♩ + ♩ =

29. 𝅗𝅥. + 𝅗𝅥. + 𝅝 + 𝅗𝅥. =

30. 𝅝 + ♩ + 𝅗𝅥. + ♫ + 𝅗𝅥 =

31. (𝅝 + 𝅗𝅥. + 𝅗𝅥) + (𝅗𝅥 + ♫ + ♬♬) =

32. (♫ + ♩) + (𝅝 + 𝅗𝅥. + 𝅗𝅥) =

33. (𝅗𝅥 + ♩) + ♫♫ =

34. 𝅗𝅥 + ♩ =

35. 𝅗𝅥 + (𝅝 + 𝅗𝅥. + ♩) =

36. (𝅗𝅥. + 𝅗𝅥.) + ♫♫ =

37. 𝄾 + (𝅝 + ♩) =

38. 𝅝 + (𝅗𝅥. + 𝅝 + ♩) =

39. (𝅝 + ♩) + 𝄽 =

40. (𝅗𝅥. + ♩ + 𝅗𝅥.) + 𝄼 =

41. 𝄽 + 𝄼 + 𝄾 =

42. 𝅝 + 𝄼 + 𝄽 =

43. 𝅗𝅥. + 𝄾 =

44. ♩ + 𝄾 + ♩. + 𝄾 =

45. ♩ + 𝄼 + 𝄾 =

46. 𝄽 + (♩. + ♩. + ♩.) =

47. 𝄼 + (𝅝 + ♩) =

48. 𝄽 + ♩. =

49. (𝅝 + 𝅝) + 𝄼 =

50. ♩ + (𝄼 + ♩.) =

51. 𝄼 + 𝄽 =

52. ♫ + ♩ + 𝄼 + ♩. + 𝄽 =

53. ♩. + 𝄾♪ + ♬ =

54. 𝄼 + ♩ + ♩. + ♩ + ♬ =

55. 𝅗𝅥 + 𝄾 =

56. 𝄼 + 𝅝 + 𝅗𝅥 + ♫ + 𝅘𝅥 =

57. 𝅗𝅥 + ♪ + ♪ + 𝄾 + 𝅘𝅥 =

58. 𝄼 + 𝅝 + 𝅗𝅥. + 𝅘𝅥 + ♫ =

59. 𝄾 + 𝄼 + 𝅝 =

60. 𝅝 + 𝄼 =

61. 𝅘𝅥 + 𝅗𝅥 =

62. ♫ + 𝅘𝅥 + 𝅗𝅥. + 𝄾 + ♬ =

63. 𝅘𝅥 + 𝄼 + 𝅗𝅥. + 𝅗𝅥 =

64. 𝅗𝅥 + 𝄼 + 𝅗𝅥. + ♫ + 𝄾 =

65. ♫ + 𝅝 =

66. 𝄽 + 𝅗𝅥. + ♫ + 𝅝 =

67. 𝅝 + ♩ + ‒ =

68. ♩ + 𝄾 + 𝅗𝅥. =

69. ‒ + 𝄽 + ♪ =

70. 𝄾 + 𝅗𝅥. + ‒ =

71. 𝅗𝅥. + 𝅝 + ♪♩ =

72. 𝅗𝅥 + 𝄾 + (𝅝 + ♪) =

73. ‒ + 𝅗𝅥 + ♫♪ =

74. ♪ + ♩ + ♫♪³ =

75. 𝄾 + 𝄽 + 𝅗𝅥 + ‒ =

76. 𝄽 + 𝅗𝅥. + ♩ =

77. ♪ + o + ♪♪ =

78. o + ♪ + ♫ =

79. ♩ + 𝄽 + o =

80. ♫ + ♩. + 𝄽 =

81. 𝄾♪ + o =

82. 𝅗𝅥 + (𝄽 + o + ♫) =

83. 𝄾 + (𝅗𝅥. + 𝅗𝅥 + ♫) =

84. ♪ + ♫ =

85. o + 𝅗𝅥 + 𝄾 + ♫ + ♫♫ =

86. 𝅗𝅥. + 𝄽 =

87. 𝄽 + 𝄾♪ =

88. 𝅝 + 𝅗𝅥. + 𝅘𝅥 + 𝅘𝅥𝅮𝅘𝅥𝅮 + 𝄼 =

89. 𝄺 + 𝅘𝅥𝅮𝅘𝅥𝅮 + 𝅝 =

90. 𝅘𝅥𝅘𝅥𝅘𝅥³ + 𝄿 =

91. 𝅘𝅥 + 𝅝 =

92. 𝅗𝅥. + 𝄺 =

93. 𝅘𝅥𝅮 + 𝅘𝅥𝅮𝅘𝅥𝅮 + 𝅘𝅥𝅘𝅥𝅘𝅥 =

94. 𝄼 + 𝅗𝅥. + 𝄻 + 𝅘𝅥 =

95. 𝄻 + (𝅝 + 𝅗𝅥. + 𝄼) =

96. 𝅝 + 𝄼 + 𝅗𝅥. + 𝄻 =

97. 𝄿 + 𝅝 =

98. 𝅘𝅥𝅮𝅘𝅥𝅮 + 𝅗𝅥. + (𝅝 + 𝅘𝅥) =

99. ♩ + 𝄾 =

100. ♪ + ♪♪♪ (3) + 𝄽 + 𝄾 + ♩. + 𝄼 =

<u>SUBTRACTION</u>

1. 𝅝 - 𝅗𝅥 =

2. 𝅘𝅥 - 𝅘𝅥𝅮 =

3. 𝅗𝅥 - 𝅘𝅥 =

4. 𝅗𝅥. - 𝅘𝅥𝅮 =

5. 𝅘𝅥 - 𝅘𝅥𝅮𝅘𝅥𝅮 =

6. 𝅘𝅥𝅮 - 𝅘𝅥𝅮 =

7. 𝅝 - 𝅗𝅥. =

8. 𝅗𝅥 - 𝅘𝅥𝅮𝅘𝅥𝅮 =

9. 𝅘𝅥 - 𝅘𝅥𝅮 =

10. 𝅘𝅥𝅮 - 𝅘𝅥𝅮𝅘𝅥𝅮 =

11. 𝅝 - ♪♫ =

12. 𝅗𝅥. - 𝅗𝅥 =

13. ♩ - ♪♪ =

14. 𝅝 - 𝅗𝅥. =

15. (𝅝 + 𝄼 + ♩) - (𝄼 + 𝅝) =

16. (𝅗𝅥. + 𝅗𝅥.) - 𝅗𝅥. =

17. (𝅗𝅥. + 𝅝 + ♩) - (𝅝 - 𝅗𝅥.) =

18. (𝅗𝅥. + 𝅗𝅥.) - (𝅗𝅥. + 𝅗𝅥.) =

19. (𝄼 + 𝄾) - (♩ + 𝄾) =

20. (𝅝 + 𝄼 + ♫) - 𝅗𝅥 =

21. (𝅝 + 𝅗𝅥.) - 𝅗𝅥. =

22. (♩ + ♫ + 𝄾) - (♩ + ♪) =

23. (♩. + 𝄼 + ♩) - (♩ + 𝅝 + ♬ + ♪) =

24. ♩ - (♩. + 𝅝) =

25. (♩. + ♩ + ♪) - 𝄾♪ =

26. ♫ - ♪ =

27. (𝅝 * 𝅝 + ♩.) - (♩. * ♩. + 𝅝) =

28. ♩ - ♪ =

29. 𝅝 - (♩ + 𝄾) =

30. ♩. - ♪ =

31. (♫ + 𝄽) – ♩ =

32. (♩. + 𝄼) – (♩ + ♩. + 𝄾♪) =

33. (♬♪ * 𝅝 + ♪) – ♩. =

34. (𝅝 * 𝄼 * 𝅝) – (♩. * 𝅝 * ♩) =

35. 𝄽 – 𝄾 – 𝄾 =

36. 𝅝 – ♩. – 𝄾 – 𝄾 =

37. (♫ – ♬♬) + (𝄽 – ♪) =

38. ♩. – ♩ – ♩ =

39. (♬♪ – 𝄽) + (𝄼 – ♪) =

40. $(\mathbf{o} + ♪) - (♩ + ♪) =$

41. $♩ - ♪ =$

42. $♩ - ♫ =$

43. $(♩. + ♪) - (𝄽 + ♼) =$

44. $(- + ♼) - (♩. + ♼) =$

45. $♩. - (♩ + ♪) =$

46. $(𝄽 + ♪) - ♪ =$

47. $(♩. + ♼) - (♩ + ♪) =$

48. $(\mathbf{o} + ♪) - ♫♪ =$

49. ($\cdot$ * $\cdot$) - (o + ♪) =

50. o^2 - (^{2} + ♪) =

51. (* $\cdot$) - ($\cdot$ * $\cdot$ +) =

52. (o + + ♪) - ($\cdot$ + ♪) =

53. ($\cdot$ +) - ♪ =

54. ($\cdot$ * $\cdot$) - - ♪ =

55. o - ♪ - - ♪ - =

56. - =

57. ($\cdot$ *) - (^{3} + ♪) =

58. $(\,\text{𝅗𝅥.} * \text{𝅗𝅥.}\,) - (\,\text{𝅗𝅥} + \text{𝄿}\,) - \text{𝄿} - \text{♪} =$

59. $(\,\text{𝅗𝅥.} + \text{♪}\,) - \text{♪} - \text{𝄾} =$

60. $\text{𝅝}^2 - (\,\text{𝅝} * \text{𝅗𝅥} + \text{𝅘𝅥}\,) - (\,\text{𝄼} + \text{♪}\,) =$

61. $(\,\text{𝅝}^2 + \text{♪}\,) - (\,\text{𝅗𝅥.}^2 + \text{♪}\,) =$

62. $(\,\text{𝅗𝅥.} + \text{𝅝} + \text{𝄼}\,) - \text{𝅗𝅥} =$

63. $(\,\text{𝅗𝅥.} * \text{𝅗𝅥.}\,) - (\,\text{𝄼} + \text{𝄼} + \text{𝄾}\,) =$

64. $(\,\text{𝅗𝅥.} + \text{𝄼}\,) - \text{𝅘𝅥} =$

65. $\text{𝅗𝅥.} - \text{𝅗𝅥} =$

66. $(\,\text{𝅝} + \text{𝅗𝅥.}\,) - \text{𝅝} =$

67. ($\half$ * $\dottedhalf$) - ($\whole$ + $\quarter$) =

68. ($\wholerest$ * $\eighth$) - ($\dottedhalf$ + $\half$) =

69. $\whole$ - $\wholerest$ =

70. ($\dottedhalf$ + $\dottedhalf$) - $\half$ =

71. ($\wholerest$ * $\dottedhalf$) ($\halfrest$ + $\dottedhalf$) =

72. ($\dottedhalf$ * $\half$ + $\halfrest$) - $\dottedhalf$ =

73. ($\whole$ * $\dottedhalf$) - ($\whole$ * $\half$) =

74. ($\dottedhalf$ * $\half$) - $\dottedhalf$ =

75. ($\dottedhalf$ * $\dottedhalf$) - ($\half$ + $\quarter$ + $\twoeighths$ + $\eighthrest$) =

76. $(\mathbf{o} + \text{𝄽}) - \text{♫♫} =$

77. $(\text{▬} + \text{♪}) - (\text{𝅗𝅥} + \text{𝄽}) =$

78. $\text{𝅗𝅥.} - \text{♩} =$

79. $\text{𝅗𝅥} - \text{𝄽} =$

80. $\mathbf{o} - \text{𝅗𝅥.} =$

81. $(\text{𝅗𝅥.} * \text{♪}) - \text{▬} =$

82. $\text{𝅗𝅥.} - \text{𝅗𝅥.} =$

83. $\text{▬} - \text{𝅗𝅥} =$

84. $\mathbf{o} - \text{▬} =$

85. (𝅝 * ♩.) − (𝅗𝅥. * ♪) =

86. (♩ + 𝅝) − 𝄽 =

87. (♫ + ▬) − (♬ + 𝅗𝅥 + ♪) =

88. (𝅗𝅥. + 𝅗𝅥. + ♪) − 𝅝 =

89. (𝅝 * ♪) − (♫ + ♬) =

90. (♩ + 𝅝 + ♫) − (𝅗𝅥. * ♪) =

91. (▬ + 𝄽) − 𝄾♪ =

92. (𝅝 * ♩.) − (𝅝 * ♩ + ♪) =

93. (𝅗𝅥 * ▬) − 𝄽 =

94. $\dotted{\halfnote}$ - $\eighthnote$ =

95. ($\quarternote$ + $\dotted{\halfnote}$) - $\eighthnote$ =

96. ($\eighthnote$ + $\eighthrest$) - $\eighthrest$ =

97. ($\eighthnote$ + $\dotted{\halfnote}$) - $\halfnote$ =

98. ($\wholenote$ + $\dotted{\halfnote}$ * $\halfnote$) - ($\quarternote$ + $\halfrest$) =

99. ($\quarternote$ + $\dotted{\halfnote}$) - ($\dotted{\halfnote}$ + $\eighthnote$) =

100. $\dotted{\halfnote}$ - $\eighthnote$ =

MULTIPLICATION

1. $(\textbf{d.} + \textbf{d.}) * (\textbf{d.} + \textbf{d}) =$

2. $(\textbf{o} + \textbf{o}) * \textbf{d.} =$

3. $(\textbf{d.} + \textbf{d.}) * (\textbf{o} + \textbf{d}) =$

4. $\textbf{—} * (\textbf{o} + \textbf{o}) =$

5. $(\textbf{d.} + \textbf{—}) * \textbf{o} =$

6. $(\textbf{o} + \textbf{d.}) * (\textbf{d.} + \textbf{d} + \textbf{♪}) =$

7. $(\textbf{—} + \textbf{♪}) * \textbf{d.} =$

8. $\textbf{d} + \textbf{—} =$

24

9. 𝅝 * (𝅝 + 𝄼 + ♪) =

𝅗𝅥. * 𝄽 =

10. (♩ + 𝅝 + 𝄼) * (♫ + 𝅗𝅥 + 𝅗𝅥 + 𝅝) =

11. ♩ * (𝅝 + ♪) =

12. 𝅝 * 𝅗𝅥 =

13. (𝄼 + 𝅗𝅥.) * (𝅗𝅥. + 𝅝) =

14. 𝅝 * (𝅝 + 𝅝 + ♪) =

15. 𝅗𝅥. * 𝅝 =

16. 𝄽 * 𝅗𝅥 =

17. $(\mathbf{o} + \mathbf{o}) * (\mathbf{o} + \text{𝅗𝅥.}) =$

18. $\text{♩} * \text{𝄾} =$

19. $(\text{𝅗𝅥.} + \text{𝅗𝅥}) * (\text{𝅗𝅥.} + \text{𝅗𝅥.}) =$

20. $\text{𝅗𝅥.} * (\mathbf{o} + \text{𝅗𝅥}) =$

21. $\text{𝄼} * (\mathbf{o} + \text{𝄼}) =$

22. $\mathbf{o} * (\text{𝄻} + \text{𝅗𝅥} + \text{♩} + \text{♫}) =$

23. $\text{𝅗𝅥.} * (\text{𝅗𝅥} + \text{𝄼}) =$

24. $\text{𝅗𝅥} * \text{♩} =$

25. $\text{𝅗𝅥.} * \text{𝅗𝅥.} =$

26. (𝅝 + ♩) * (𝅗𝅥. + 𝅝 + ♩) =

27. (𝅝 + 𝅗𝅥. + 𝅖) * ♩ =

28. (𝅗𝅥. + 𝅗𝅥 + 𝄽 + ♪) * 𝅗𝅥. =

29. 𝅗𝅥 * 𝅗𝅥. =

30. 𝄽 * ♫ =

31. (𝅗𝅥. + ♩) * (𝅝 + 𝅗𝅥.) =

32. (𝅗𝅥. + 𝅗𝅥.) * 𝅗𝅥 =

33. (𝅝 + ♩ + 𝅝) * 𝅗𝅥. =

34. (𝄽 + 𝅖) * (𝅗𝅥. + 𝅝 + ♩) =

35. (o + o) * (𝅗𝅥. + 𝅗𝅥) =

36. o * 𝅗𝅥. =

37. (𝄼 + 𝅗𝅥. + ♩) * 𝅗𝅥. =

38. (o + 𝄿 + 𝄼) * (♫ + 𝄼 + o + ♩) =

39. ♩ * (o + 𝅗𝅥.) =

40. (o + 𝅗𝅥.) * (𝅗𝅥 + 𝅗𝅥.) =

41. (𝅗𝅥. + 𝄼) * (o + 𝅗𝅥. + ♩ + ♫) =

42. ♩ * (𝅗𝅥. + 𝅗𝅥) =

43. o * o =

44. 𝅗𝅥. * (𝅗𝅥. + 𝄿 + o) =

45. (♫ + ♬) * (o + 𝅗𝅥.) =

46. ($\mathcal{d}.$ + $\mathcal{d}.$) * ($\rule{3mm}{0.4mm}$ + $\mathcal{d}$) =

47. $\mathcal{d}$ * (ξ + $\mathbf{o}$) =

48. $\rule{3mm}{0.4mm}$ * ($\mathcal{d}$ + $\mathcal{JJ}$) =

49. ($\mathbf{o}$ + $\mathcal{d}$ + $\rule{3mm}{0.4mm}$) * ($\mathcal{d}.$ + ξ) =

50. $\mathbf{o}$ * $\mathbf{o}$ =

51. $\mathcal{d}$ * ($\mathbf{o}$ + $\mathbf{o}$) =

52. ($\mathcal{d}.$ + $\mathcal{JJ}$ + $\mathbf{o}$ + ξ) * $\mathcal{d}$ =

53. $\mathcal{d}.$ * $\rule{3mm}{0.4mm}$ =

54. $\mathbf{o}$ * ξ =

55. $\mathcal{d}.$ * ($\mathcal{JJJ}$ + $\rule{3mm}{0.4mm}$ + $\mathcal{d}.$ + $\mathcal{\gamma J}$) =

56. ($\rule{3mm}{0.4mm}$ + $\mathcal{d}$ + $\rule{3mm}{0.4mm}$) * ($\mathcal{d}.$ + $\mathbf{o}$) =

57. (𝅗𝅥. + 𝅝) * 𝅝 =

58. 𝅘𝅥 * 𝅗𝅥. =

59. 𝄼 * 𝅗𝅥 =

60. (𝅝 + 𝅝) * 𝅗𝅥. =

61. (𝄻 + 𝄾 + 𝅝) * (𝅝 + 𝅘𝅥𝅮𝅘𝅥𝅮 + 𝅝) =

62. (𝅗𝅥 + 𝅗𝅥 + 𝅘𝅥𝅮𝅘𝅥𝅮 + 𝅝) * 𝅝 =

63. (𝅗𝅥 + 𝅘𝅥𝅮) * (𝅝 + 𝅗𝅥.) =

64. (𝄻 + 𝄼 + 𝄿𝅘𝅥𝅮) * (𝅘𝅥𝅮𝅘𝅥𝅮 + 𝅗𝅥. + 𝅗𝅥.) =

65. 𝄾 * 𝅘𝅥 =

66. (𝅝 + 𝅘𝅥𝅮) * (𝅗𝅥. + 𝅝) =

67. 𝅗𝅥 * 𝅗𝅥. =

68. ♩. * (𝅝 + ♪) =

69. (𝄼 + 𝄽) * (⁷♪ + 𝅝 + ♩. + 𝄽) =

70. (♫♬ + 𝅝 + ♪) * ♩ =

71. ♩. * 𝅝 =

72. (𝅝 + ♩.) * (♩ + 𝄼 + ♩.) =

73. ♩ * ♩ =

74. 𝅝 * (♩. + ♩ + ♪) =

75. (𝄼 + ♫ + ♪) * (⁷♬ + ♩.) =

76. (𝅝 + ♬♬) * ♩ =

77. (♩ + ♪) * (𝅝 + ♩. + ♫) =

78. ♩ * 𝅝 =

79. 𝄾 * ♩ =

80. (𝅗𝅥. + ♩ + ♪) * (𝅗𝅥. + ♪) =

81. (♬ + 𝅗𝅥. + 𝅗𝅥 + ♪) * 𝄽 =

82. (𝅗𝅥. + ♪.) * (𝅗𝅥. + ♪) =

83. (𝅗𝅥 + ♪.) * (𝅝 + 𝅝) =

84. 𝅝 * 𝅗𝅥. =

85. (𝄾♪) * (𝅗𝅥 + ♫ + ♬) =

86. (𝅝 + 𝅝) * (𝅝 + 𝅝) =

87. 𝅗𝅥 * (𝅗𝅥. + 𝅝) =

88. (♫ + 𝅗𝅥. + 𝅝) * (♫ + ♬ + 𝅗𝅥 + 𝅗𝅥. + 𝄼) =

89. (𝅝 + 𝄽) * (♫ + 𝄾♪ + ♪ + 𝅗𝅥.) =

90. (𝅝 + ♫ + 𝅝) * (𝅗𝅥 + 𝅗𝅥. + 𝅗𝅥) =

91. 𝅗𝅥 * 𝅝 =

92. (𝅗𝅥. + 𝅗𝅥) * 𝄽 =

93. ♩ * (𝅗𝅥. + 𝅗𝅥.) =

94. 𝅝 * (𝅝 + 𝅗𝅥.) =

95. 𝅗𝅥. * (𝅝 + 𝅝) =

96. 𝅗𝅥. * 𝅗𝅥 =

97. 𝄾♪ * (𝅗𝅥 + 𝄽 + 𝅝 + ♫ + ♩) =

98. (𝅜 + 𝄺 + 𝅗𝅥.) * (♫ + 𝅝 + ♬ + 𝄽) =

99. (♫ + 𝄾♪) * (𝄾♪ + ♩) =

DIVISION

1. 𝅗𝅥 ÷ ♪ =

2. 𝅝 ÷ 𝅘𝅥 =

3. (𝅗𝅥 + 𝄽) ÷ (𝅝 + 𝅗𝅥) =

4. (𝅝 * 𝅗𝅥.) ÷ 𝅗𝅥 =

5. (𝄽 + 𝅘𝅥𝅮) * 𝅝 ÷ (𝅗𝅥. + 𝅘𝅥) =

6. (𝅘𝅥𝅮𝅘𝅥𝅮 + 𝅝) * (𝄽 + 𝅘𝅥) ÷ 𝅗𝅥. =

7. (𝅝 * 𝅗𝅥. * 𝅗𝅥.) ÷ 𝅝 =

8. (𝅗𝅥. * 𝅝) ÷ 𝄽 =

9. (𝄽 * 𝅗𝅥.) ÷ (𝅗𝅥 + 𝅘𝅥) =

10. (𝅗𝅥. * 𝅗𝅥.) ÷ 𝅗𝅥. =

11. (♩ + ♩ + 𝅗𝅥.) * 𝅗𝅥. ÷ (𝅝 + ♩) =

12. 𝄼 ÷ 𝅗𝅥 =

13. 𝅗𝅥 * (𝅗𝅥. + 𝅗𝅥) ÷ 𝄻 =

14. (𝄼 + 𝅗𝅥. * 𝅗𝅥.) ÷ (𝅗𝅥 + ♪) =

15. ♩ ÷ 𝅗𝅥 =

16. (𝅗𝅥. + 𝅗𝅥. * 𝅗𝅥.) ÷ (𝅝 + 𝄼 + ♪) =

17. (𝅝 * 𝅗𝅥 * 𝅝) ÷ (𝅝 + 𝅝) =

18. ____ ÷ (𝅗𝅥. * 𝅗𝅥 + ♪) = (𝅗𝅥. * 𝅗𝅥)

19. ____ ÷ 𝅝 = (𝅝 + ♪)

20. ____ ÷ (𝅝 + 𝄼) = 𝅗𝅥.

21. ____ ÷ (𝄻 * 𝅗𝅥 + ♪) = (𝅗𝅥. * 𝅗𝅥 + ♪)

22. ____ ÷ 𝄻 = (𝅗𝅥. * 𝄼 + 𝄽)

23. ____ ÷ (𝄻 + 𝄽) = 0

24. ____ ÷ (𝅝 * 𝅗𝅥 + 𝅗𝅥.) = (𝄻 * 𝄼 + 𝅗𝅥.)

25. ____ ÷ (𝅗𝅥. * 𝅘𝅥) = (𝅗𝅥 * 𝅗𝅥. * 𝄼)

26. ____ ÷ 𝅝 = (𝅗𝅥 + 𝅘𝅥)

27. ____ ÷ (𝅝 + ♪) = 𝅝

28. ____ ÷ 𝅗𝅥. = (𝅝 + 𝅗𝅥.)

29. ____ ÷ 𝄻 = (𝅝 + 𝅝 + ♪)

30. (𝅝 * 𝅗𝅥.) ÷ 𝅝 =

31. ____ ÷ 𝅗𝅥. = (𝅝 + 𝅘𝅥 + 𝄻)

32. (𝅗𝅥. * 𝅝) ÷ 𝅗𝅥. =

33. ____ ÷ (𝅗𝅥. * 𝅗𝅥 + ♪) = (𝅗𝅥. * 𝅗𝅥.)

34. ____ ÷ (𝅝 * 𝅗𝅥) = (𝅝 + 𝄽)

35. ____ ÷ (▬ * ▬) = 𝅝

36. (𝅗𝅥. * 𝅗𝅥.) ÷ 𝅗𝅥. =

37. ____ ÷ (𝅝 + ♪) = 𝅗𝅥

38. ____ ÷ (𝅗𝅥. + 𝅗𝅥.) = 𝅗𝅥.

39. ____ ÷ (𝅗𝅥. * 𝅗𝅥 + ♪) = (𝅝 * 𝅗𝅥)

40. ____ ÷ (𝅗𝅥. * ▬ + 𝄽) = (𝅗𝅥. + 𝅗𝅥.)

41. ____ ÷ (♩ + 𝅝) = (𝅗𝅥. + ♪)

42. (𝅝 * 𝅝) ÷ 𝅝 =

43. (𝅝 * 𝅝) ÷ 𝅗𝅥 =

44. _____ ÷ 𝅗𝅥 = 𝅝

45. (𝅗𝅥. * 𝅗𝅥) ÷ 𝅗𝅥 =

46. _____ ÷ (𝅝 * 𝅗𝅥 + ♪) = 𝅗𝅥

47. 𝅝 ÷ 𝅗𝅥 =

48. (𝅗𝅥. * 𝅝) ÷ (𝅗𝅥. * 𝅗𝅥) =

49. (𝅗𝅥 * 𝅗𝅥. + 𝄾) ÷ ♫ =

50. (𝅝 * 𝄻) ÷ (♬ + ♫) =

51. _____ ÷ 𝅗𝅥. = (♫ + 𝅗𝅥)

52. _____ ÷ (𝅗𝅥. * 𝅗𝅥 + ♬) = (𝅗𝅥. * 𝅗𝅥)

53. _____ ÷ 𝅗𝅥 = (𝅝 + ♫ + 𝅝)

54. (𝅝 * 𝄻) ÷ ♫ =

55. ___ ÷ (♪♪♪ + ♪♪) = (𝅝 + 𝅝)

56. ___ ÷ (𝅗𝅥. * ♪) = (𝄽 * 𝄼)

57. ___ ÷ 𝅝 =

58. 𝅗𝅥 ÷ 𝄼 =

59. ___ ÷ 𝅗𝅥. = (𝅝 + 𝄼 + 𝄾)

60. ___ ÷ (𝅗𝅥 + ♪) = (𝅗𝅥. * ♪)

61. (𝅗𝅥. + ♩ + 𝅗𝅥) ÷ (♪♪ + 𝄿♪ + 𝄾) =

62. (𝅝 * 𝅗𝅥) ÷ (𝅗𝅥. + 𝄾) =

63. ___ ÷ (𝄼 * 𝅝) = (𝅝 + ♪♪)

64. 𝅝 ÷ (𝅗𝅥. + 𝄿♪) =

65. ___ ÷ (♩ + 𝄿♪) = (𝅗𝅥. + 𝅝)

66. ___ ÷ (𝅗𝅥. * ♪) = (𝅗𝅥 * 𝅗𝅥.)

67. ___ ÷ (𝅝 + 𝅗𝅥.) = (𝅝 * 𝅗𝅥 + 𝄾)

68. ___ ÷ (𝄼 + 𝄾♪) = 𝅗𝅥.

69. ___ ÷ (𝅝 + 𝅗𝅥.) = (𝅝 * 𝅗𝅥 + ♪)

70. ___ ÷ (♫ + 𝅝 * 𝅗𝅥 - ♪) = (𝅗𝅥. + 𝅝)

71. (𝅗𝅥 * ♪) ÷ (𝅗𝅥. + ♫) =

72. (𝅝 * 𝅗𝅥.) ÷ (𝅗𝅥 + ♪) =

73. 𝅗𝅥 ÷ 𝅗𝅥 =

74. ___ ÷ 𝅝 = (𝄼 * 𝄻)

75. ___ ÷ (𝅗𝅥. * 𝅗𝅥.) = 𝅗𝅥

76. ___ ÷ (𝅝 + 𝅗𝅥.) = (𝅗𝅥. * ♪)

77. ___ ÷ (𝅗𝅥 + 𝅗𝅥 + 𝅗𝅥.) = 𝅗𝅥.

78. (𝅝 * ♪) ÷ (𝅗𝅥 * 𝅝) =

79. ___ ÷ 𝅝 = 𝅝

80. ___ ÷ (𝅗𝅥. * 𝅗𝅥.) = (𝅝 + 𝅗𝅥 + ♪)

81. ___ ÷ 𝅗𝅥 = (𝅗𝅥. + 𝅗𝅥)

82. ___ ÷ (𝅗𝅥. * 𝅗𝅥 + 𝅗𝅥.) = 𝅗𝅥

83. (𝅗𝅥. * 𝅗𝅥) ÷ 𝅗𝅥 =

84. ___ ÷ 𝅝 = (𝅗𝅥. * 𝅗𝅥.)

85. ___ ÷ (𝅗𝅥. + 𝅗𝅥) = 𝅗𝅥.

86. ___ ÷ (𝅗𝅥. * 𝅗𝅥) = (𝅝 + 𝅝)

87. (𝅝 + 𝅝) ÷ 𝅘𝅥 =

88. ___ ÷ (𝅝 * ♪) = (𝅗𝅥 * 𝅝)

89. ($𝅝$ + $𝅗𝅥.$ + $♪$) ÷ _____ = $♩$

90. _____ ÷ $𝅗𝅥$ = ($𝅗𝅥.$ * $♪$) + $♩$

91. _____ ÷ ($𝅝$ * $♪$) = ($𝅗𝅥.$ * $♪$)

92. _____ ÷ ($𝅗𝅥$ * $𝅗𝅥.$) = ($𝅝$ + $♪$)

93. _____ ÷ ($𝅝$ + $♩$) = ($𝅝$ + $𝅗𝅥.$ + $♪$)

94. _____ ÷ ($𝅗𝅥.$ * $𝅗𝅥.$) = ($𝅗𝅥.$ + $♪$)

95. ($𝅝$ + $𝅝$) ÷ $𝅝$ =

96. _____ ÷ $𝅗𝅥$ = ($𝅝$ + $♩$)

97. _____ ÷ ($𝅗𝅥.$ * $𝅗𝅥$ + $𝅗𝅥.$) = ($𝅗𝅥.$ * $𝅗𝅥$ + $♩$)

98. _____ ÷ $𝅝$ = $𝅝$

99. _____ ÷ ($𝅝$ + $𝅝$) = $𝅝$

100. _____ ÷ ($𝅝$ + $𝅗𝅥.$) = $𝅗𝅥.$

EXPONENTS

1. $\mathbf{o}^2 + \text{𝅗𝅥.}^2 =$

2. $\text{𝅘𝅥}^3 - \text{𝅘𝅥}^3 =$

3. $\text{▬}^1 - \text{𝅘𝅥}^2 =$

4. $(\text{𝅗𝅥} + \text{𝅘𝅥})^3 - \text{𝅘𝅥𝅮}^2 =$

5. $(\mathbf{o} + \text{𝅘𝅥𝅮})^2 + (\text{𝅗𝅥.} + \text{𝅘𝅥𝅮})^3 - \text{𝅘𝅥𝅮}$

6. $\text{𝅘𝅥𝅮}^2 + \text{𝅘𝅥𝅮}^2 =$

7. $\text{𝅗𝅥.}^3 - \text{𝅘𝅥}^2 =$

8. $\text{𝅘𝅥𝅮}^1 + (\text{𝅘𝅥𝅮𝅘𝅥𝅮} - \text{𝅘𝅥𝅮}) =$

9. $\text{𝅘𝅥}^2 * (\text{𝅗𝅥.} + \text{𝅘𝅥𝅮}) =$

10. $\mathbf{o}^2 \div \mathbf{o} =$

11. ♪¹ + (𝅗𝅥 + 𝅝 − 𝅗𝅥.) =

12. (𝅗𝅥² * ♪) + 𝅘𝅥. − (♩ * 𝅝) − ♪ =

13. 𝅝² ÷ (♫♪ + ♪) + 𝅘𝅥. * 𝅗𝅥 − ♪ =

14. 𝅘𝅥.³ =

15. 𝅗𝅥³ =

16. (𝅘𝅥. + ♪)² =

17. (𝅝 * 𝅘𝅥.)² =

18. (𝅝 * 𝅗𝅥 + 𝅗𝅥)² =

19. (𝅝 * ♪)³ =

20. (♩ * 𝅝)² =

21. (𝅘𝅥. * ▬)² =

22. (𝅘𝅥. * 𝅗𝅥 + 𝄽)² =

23. $\quad \text{♩}^3 =$

24. $(\text{♩.} \ast \rule[0.5ex]{1em}{0.4pt})^2 =$

25. $\text{♩.}^3 =$

26. $\text{♩}^3 =$

27. $\text{♩.}^2 =$

28. $(\rule[0.5ex]{1em}{0.4pt} + \text{♫})^2 =$

29. $(\text{o} + \text{♩.} + \text{♪})^3 =$

30. $(\text{♩.} + \text{o})^3 =$

31. $(\text{♩.} \ast \text{♩.})^2 =$

32. $\text{♩.}^3 =$

33. $(\text{o} \ast \text{o})^2 =$

34. $(\text{♩.} \ast \text{♩.})^2 =$

35. $(\mathbf{o} + \xi)^2 =$

36. $\mathbf{o}^3 =$

37. $\flat^1 =$

38. $\flat_{\cdot}{}^2 =$

39. $(\flat_{\cdot} + \flat)^2 =$

40. $\flat_{\cdot}{}^2 =$

41. $(\flat_{\cdot} + \flat * \flat)^2 =$

42. $(\mathbf{o} + \flat_{\cdot})^3 =$

43. $(\flat_{\cdot} * \flat_{\cdot})2 =$

44. $(\flat_{\cdot} * \flat)2 =$

45. $(\flat_{\cdot} * \flat_{\cdot})^2 =$

46. $\mathbf{o}^2 =$

47. $(\half + \eighth)^3 =$

48. $(\whole * \half)^3 =$

49. $(\dottedhalf * \half)^2$

50. $(\quarter + \rest)^3 =$

51. $(\dottedhalf + \eighthgroup)^1 =$

52. $(\dottedhalf - \eighthgroup)^2 =$

53. $(\whole + \whole)^2 =$

54. $(\half * \dottedhalf) * \quarter\ ^3 =$

55. $(\dottedhalf * \dottedhalf)^3 =$

56. $\whole^{1/2} =$

57. $\half^2 =$

58. $\left(\text{𝅗𝅥.} + \text{𝅗𝅥} \right)^2 =$

59. $\left(\text{o} * \text{♩} \right) * \left(\text{𝅗𝅥} * \text{o} \right)^2 =$

60. $\left(\text{o} * \text{𝅗𝅥} \right)^2 =$

61. $\left(\text{𝅗𝅥.} * \text{𝅗𝅥.} \right)^3 =$

62. $\text{𝅗𝅥.}^1 =$

63. $\left(\text{o} + \text{♩} \right)^2 =$

64. $\left(\text{𝅗𝅥.} * \text{—} \right)^2 =$

65. $\left(\text{—} * \text{♩} \right)^2 =$

66. $\left(\text{𝅗𝅥.} * \text{♩} \right)^2 =$

67. $\text{o}^3 =$

68. $\left(\text{o} * \text{𝅗𝅥.} \right)^2 =$

69. $(\text{𝅗𝅥.} + \text{𝅗𝅥} * \text{♩})^2 =$

70. $\text{♩}^3 =$

71. $(\text{𝅗𝅥.} * \text{𝅗𝅥.})^3 =$

72. $(\text{𝅗𝅥.} * \text{𝅗𝅥})^2 =$

73. $(\text{𝅝} * \text{𝅗𝅥})^2 =$

74. $(\text{♩} + \text{♫} + \text{♫♪})^3 =$

75. $\text{♩} + \text{𝅝}^2 =$

76. $(\text{𝅝} + \text{♪})^3 =$

77. $(\text{𝅗𝅥.} * \text{𝅗𝅥}) + \text{♩}^3 =$

78. $(\text{𝅝} + \text{♪})^1 =$

79. $(\text{𝅝} + \text{𝅗𝅥.})^3 =$

80. $\left(\raisebox{0pt}{𝅗𝅥.}\right)^3 =$

81. $\left(𝅝 * 𝅗𝅥.\right)^2 =$

82. $𝅗𝅥 + 𝅘𝅥\ ^1 =$

83. $\left(𝅗𝅥 * 𝅗𝅥\right)^3 =$

84. $𝅗𝅥^3 =$

85. $\left(𝅗𝅥. * 𝅗𝅥.\right)^3 =$

86. $\left(𝅘𝅥 + 𝅘𝅥\right)$

87. $\left(𝅝 * 𝅗𝅥\right)^2 =$

88. $\left(𝅝 + 𝅘𝅥\right)^2 =$

89. $𝅝^3 =$

90. $\left(𝅝 + 𝅘𝅥 * 𝅗𝅥\right)^2 =$

91. $\left(𝅘𝅥 + 𝅝\right)^3 =$

92. $\left(\text{𝅗𝅥.}\right)^3 =$

93. $\left(\text{𝅗𝅥.} \; * \; \text{♪}\right)^2 =$

94. $\left(\text{𝅗𝅥.} \; - \; \text{♪}\right)^3 =$

95. $\left(\text{𝅗𝅥.}\right)^2 =$

96. $\left(\text{𝅗𝅥.} \; * \; \text{𝅗𝅥.}\right)^3 =$

97. $\left(\text{𝅝} \; + \; \text{𝅝} \; + \; \text{♪}\right)^2 =$

98. $\left(\text{𝅝} \; + \; \text{𝅗𝅥.}\right)^3 =$

99. $\left(\text{𝅝} \; + \; \text{𝅝}\right)^3 =$

100. $\left(\text{𝅗𝅥}\right)^3 =$

SQUARE ROOTS (RADICALS)

1. $\sqrt{(\text{𝅗𝅥.} * \text{𝅗𝅥.})} =$

2. $(\text{𝅝} + \text{𝅗𝅥.}) - (\text{♩} + \text{♫♫}) * \text{♩} \div \text{♩} * \sqrt{(\text{𝅗𝅥.} * \text{𝅗𝅥.})} =$

3. $\sqrt{\underline{\quad}} = \text{𝅗𝅥.}$

4. $\sqrt{\underline{\quad}} = (\text{𝅗𝅥.} + \text{♩})^2$

5. $\sqrt{\underline{\quad}} = (\text{𝅝} * \text{♩} + \text{𝄽})$

6. $\sqrt{\underline{\quad}} = (\text{𝅝} * \text{♩})$

7. $\sqrt{\underline{\quad}} = \text{𝅝}^2$

8. $\sqrt{\underline{\quad}} = (\text{𝅝} + \text{♫})$

9. $\sqrt{\underline{\quad}} = (\text{𝅝} + \text{♩})$

10. $\sqrt{\underline{\quad}} = (\text{𝅝} * \text{♩.})$

11. $\sqrt{(𝅝 + 𝅗𝅥.)^2}$ =

12. $\sqrt{(𝅝 * 𝅗𝅥. + 𝅝)}$ =

13. $\sqrt{(𝅗𝅥. * 𝅗𝅥)^2}$ =

14. $\sqrt{}$ = 𝅗𝅥.$\sqrt{(𝅗𝅥. + 𝅗𝅥)}$

15. $\sqrt{}$ = (𝅝 * 𝅗𝅥)$\sqrt{𝅗𝅥}$

16. $\sqrt{}$ = (𝅗𝅥. + 𝅗𝅥)$\sqrt{(𝅗𝅥. * 𝅗𝅥)}$

17. $\sqrt{}$ = (𝅝 * 𝅗𝅥 + 𝅗𝅥.)$\sqrt{(𝅝 + 𝅗𝅥.)}$

18. $\sqrt{}$ = 𝅗𝅥$\sqrt{(𝅗𝅥 + 𝅝)}$

19. $\sqrt{}$ = (𝅝 + 𝅝 + 𝅗𝅥)$\sqrt{𝅗𝅥.}$

20. $\sqrt{}$ = 𝅝$\sqrt{(𝅗𝅥. + 𝅝)}$

21. $\sqrt{}$ = (𝅗𝅥 * 𝅗𝅥.)$\sqrt{(𝅗𝅥 + 𝅝)}$

22. $\sqrt{}$ = (𝅝 * 𝅗𝅥 + 𝅗𝅥)$\sqrt{𝅗𝅥}$

23. √_____ = 𝅝

24. √_____ = (𝅝 * 𝅝 + ♪)

25. √_____ = (𝅗𝅥. + ♪ * 𝅗𝅥)

26. √_____ = (𝅝 + 𝅗𝅥. + 𝅝)

27. √_____ = (𝅗𝅥 * 𝅗𝅥.)

28. √𝅝 =

29. √_____ = (𝅝 + ♪)²

30. √_____ = 𝅝²

31. √_____ = (𝅗𝅥. * 𝅝 + ♪)

32. √_____ = (𝅝 * 𝅗𝅥.)

33. √_____ = (𝅗𝅥. + ♪)

34. √_____ = (♫ + 𝅗𝅥. * 𝅗𝅥. + ♬)

35. $\sqrt{}$ = (♩. + o)

36. $\sqrt{}$ = o²

37. $\sqrt{}$ = ♩.²

38. $\sqrt{}$ = (♩ * ♩.)

39. $\sqrt{}$(o * o) =

40. $\sqrt{}$(♩. * ♩.) =

41. $\sqrt{}$ = ♩

42. $\sqrt{}$ = (♩. + ♩ * ♩.)

43. ♩$\sqrt{5}$ + o$\sqrt{5}$ = (♩ + o)$\sqrt{5}$

44. $\sqrt{}$♩. + (♩. * ♩.)$\sqrt{}$♩. = ___$\sqrt{}$♩.

45. o$\sqrt{}$ + ___$\sqrt{}$(o + ♩.) = (o + o + ♩)$\sqrt{}$(o + ♩.)

46. (♩. + o)$\sqrt{}$♩ + (o + ♪)$\sqrt{}$♩ + $\sqrt{}$♩ = ___$\sqrt{}$♩

47. $\sqrt{\text{♩.}}$ + ♩.$\sqrt{\text{♩.}}$ + $\sqrt{\text{♩.}}$ = (♩. + ♪)$\sqrt{\text{♩.}}$

48. (♩.+♩.)$\sqrt{\text{(♩.+♪)}}$ + $\sqrt{\text{(♩.+♪)}}$ + $\sqrt{\text{(♩.+♪)}}$ + $\sqrt{\text{(♩.+♪)}}$ = ___ $\sqrt{\text{(♩.+♪)}}$

49. $\sqrt{\text{(♩.+o)}}$ + $\sqrt{\text{♩}}$ + $\sqrt{\text{(o+♪)}}$ + $\sqrt{\text{♩}}$ = ♪$\sqrt{\quad}$ + ♪$\sqrt{\quad}$

50. $\sqrt{\text{♩.}}$ + ♪$\sqrt{\text{♩.}}$ + $\sqrt{\text{♩}}$ = ♩.$\sqrt{\text{♩.}}$ + $\sqrt{\text{♩}}$

51. o$\sqrt{\text{♩}}$ + ___ $\sqrt{\text{♩}}$ + ♩.$\sqrt{\text{♩}}$ = (o)²$\sqrt{\text{♩}}$

52. $\sqrt{\quad}$ + (o + ♩.)$\sqrt{\quad}$ = (o + ♪)² * ♩.

53. $\sqrt{\quad}$ + (♩. * ♩.)$\sqrt{\text{♩}}$ + $\sqrt{\text{(♩. * ♩ * ♩.)}}$ = o²$\sqrt{\text{♩}}$

54. $\sqrt{45}$ + (♩. + ♩)$\sqrt{\text{(♩ + ♩. * o)}}$ + (♩. * ♩.)$\sqrt{\text{♩.}}$ + $\sqrt{75}$ =

13$\sqrt{\text{(♩ + ♩.)}}$ + 14$\sqrt{\text{♩.}}$

55. ♪$\sqrt{\text{(o * ♩)}}$ + 11$\sqrt{72}$ + $\sqrt{96}$ = 70$\sqrt{\text{♩}}$ + o$\sqrt{\text{(o + ♩)}}$

56. $\sqrt{\text{o}}$ =

57. $\sqrt{\text{(o + ♪)}^2}$ =

58. $\sqrt{𝅘𝅥.}^2 =$

59. $\sqrt{(𝅗𝅥. + 𝅝)^2} =$

60. $\sqrt{(𝅗𝅥. * 𝅗𝅥.)^2} =$

61. $\sqrt{(𝅗𝅥. * 𝅘𝅥𝅮)^2} =$

62. $\sqrt{(𝅝 * 𝅝)^2} =$

63. $\sqrt{𝅘𝅥} =$

64. $\sqrt{𝅝}^2 =$

65. $\sqrt[3]{(𝅗𝅥 * 𝅝)} =$

66. $\sqrt[3]{𝅘𝅥} =$

67. $\sqrt[3]{(𝅝 * 𝅝)^2} =$

68. $\sqrt[3]{(𝅗𝅥. + 𝅗𝅥)^3} =$

69. $\sqrt[3]{\underline{\hspace{2em}}} = 𝅗𝅥.$

70. $\sqrt[3]{}$ = 𝅝 + 𝅗𝅥.

71. $\sqrt[3]{0}$ =

72. $\sqrt[3]{}$ = 𝅗𝅥 + 𝅝

73. $\sqrt{}$(𝅗𝅥. * 𝅗𝅥. * 𝅗𝅥) =

74. $\sqrt{}$(𝅗𝅥. * 𝅗𝅥. * 𝅗𝅥.) =

75. $\sqrt{}$(𝅝 * 𝅗𝅥 * 𝅝) =

76. $\sqrt{75}$ =

77. $\sqrt{28}$ =

78. $\sqrt[3]{}$(𝅝 * 𝅝) =

79. $\sqrt[3]{}$ = 𝅗𝅥. $\sqrt[3]{}$𝅗𝅥

80. $\sqrt[3]{}$ = (𝅝 + ♩) $\sqrt[3]{}$𝅗𝅥.

81. $\sqrt[3]{}$ = 𝅝 $\sqrt[3]{}$(𝅝 + ♩)

82. $\sqrt[3]{162}=$

83. $\text{♩}\sqrt{\text{𝅗𝅥.}}+\text{♩}\sqrt{\text{𝅗𝅥.}}-\text{𝅗𝅥.}\sqrt{\text{𝅗𝅥.}}=$

84. $_7\sqrt{\text{♩}}+(\text{𝅗𝅥.}+\text{♩})\sqrt{\text{♩}}-(\text{𝅗𝅥.}*\text{♩})\sqrt{\text{♩}}=$

85. $(\text{o}*\text{♩})\sqrt{17}-\sqrt{17}+(\text{𝅗𝅥.}+\text{𝅗𝅥.})\sqrt{17}=$

86. $_{11}\sqrt{\text{𝅗𝅥.}}-\text{♩}\sqrt{11}+(\text{o}+\text{♪})\sqrt{11}=$

87. $(\text{♪}+\text{o})\sqrt{(\text{𝅗𝅥.}+\text{♩})}+\text{o}\sqrt{(\text{o}+\text{♪})}-\text{𝅗𝅥.}\sqrt{(\text{♩}+\text{𝅗𝅥.})}=$

88. $_8\sqrt{\text{♩}}+\text{o}\sqrt{\text{♩}}-\text{𝅗𝅥.}\sqrt{\text{♩}}=$

89. $_9\sqrt{11}-_8\sqrt{11}+\sqrt{11}=$

90. $_5\sqrt{\text{𝅗𝅥.}}-_5\sqrt{\text{𝅗𝅥.}}+\text{o}\sqrt{\text{♩}}=$

91. $(\text{𝅗𝅥.}*\text{♩})\sqrt{5}-\text{♩}\sqrt{\text{𝅗𝅥.}}+\text{♩}\sqrt{5}=$

92. $\sqrt{\text{𝅗𝅥.}}*\sqrt{\text{𝅗𝅥.}}=$

93. $\text{♩}\sqrt{7}*\text{𝅗𝅥.}\sqrt{7}=$

94. $\sqrt{5}*(\text{𝅗𝅥.}*\text{♩})\sqrt{5}=$

95. o $\sqrt{}$ 𝅗𝅥. * $\sqrt{}$ 𝅗𝅥. * 𝅗𝅥 $\sqrt{}$ 𝅗𝅥. =

96. 𝅗𝅥 $\sqrt{}$ 𝅗𝅥 * $\sqrt{}$ 𝅗𝅥 * $_6\sqrt{}$ 5 =

97. $_{12}\sqrt{}$ 𝅗𝅥. * 𝅗𝅥. $\sqrt{}$ 𝅗𝅥. =

98. $\sqrt{}$ 5 * 𝅗𝅥. $\sqrt{}$ 5 =

99. $_6\sqrt{}$ 𝅗𝅥 * $_9\sqrt{}$ 𝅗𝅥 =

100. $_5\sqrt{}$ 5 * 𝅗𝅥. $\sqrt{}$ 5 =

ALGEBRA

1. 𝅗𝅥. x + (𝅝 + 𝅗𝅥.) = x − 𝅗𝅥

2. 𝅝 x = 𝅗𝅥. − ♫

3. (𝅗𝅥 x + 𝅗𝅥) − (𝅝 * 𝅗𝅥.) =

4. (𝅝 + 𝅗𝅥.)

5. x − (𝅝 + 𝅗𝅥.)x =

6. x + (𝅗𝅥 + 𝅘𝅥 + 𝄽)x =

7. ___ + (𝅝 + 𝅘𝅥)x − (𝅝 * 𝅗𝅥) = ___x − (𝅗𝅥. + 𝅗𝅥 * 𝅗𝅥)

8. 𝅗𝅥 (𝅗𝅥. x − 𝅝) = 𝅗𝅥. x + 𝅘𝅥

9. 𝅗𝅥. x = 𝅗𝅥. + 𝅗𝅥 (x + 𝅗𝅥.) − 𝅗𝅥.

10. 𝅝 x + (𝅝 + 𝅗𝅥.) − (𝅗𝅥. * 𝅗𝅥)x = (𝅗𝅥. . + 𝅗𝅥) − 𝅝 x + 𝅝

11. 𝅗𝅥. (𝅗𝅥. + 𝅗𝅥 x − 𝅗𝅥) + 𝅝 x = (𝅝 * 𝅗𝅥 + 𝅘𝅥)x + (𝅗𝅥. + 𝅗𝅥.) − 𝅗𝅥 x

12. 𝅘𝅥 + 𝅗𝅥. x = 𝅗𝅥 (𝅗𝅥. x − 𝅝)

13. x + 𝅗𝅥 = 𝅗𝅥.

14. z + 𝅝 = (𝅝 + 𝄼 + ♫♪)

15. x + (𝅗𝅥. ∗ ♩) = (𝅝 ∗ 𝅗𝅥. − ♩)

16. m + ♫ = (𝅝 ∗ ♩)

17. n + 𝅗𝅥. = (𝅝 ∗ 𝅗𝅥. + ♩)

18. y + (𝅗𝅥 + ♩) = (𝅗𝅥 + 𝅗𝅥. ∗ ♩)

19. x + (𝅗𝅥. + ♩ + ♩) = (𝅝 ∗ ♩)

20. z + 𝄼 = 𝅗𝅥. ∗ ♩

21. y + 𝄼 = − ♩

22. x + ♩ = − 𝄾

23. s + (𝅗𝅥. + 𝅗𝅥.) = − 𝅝

24. z + 𝅗𝅥. = − (𝅝 ∗ ♩)

25. x + ♩ = − (𝅝 + 𝅝 + ♩)

26. y + (𝅗𝅥. + 𝅗𝅥. + ♩) = − (𝅗𝅥. ∗ ♩)

27. x + 𝅗𝅥. = (o + 𝅗𝅥.)

28. 𝅗𝅥. x = 24

29. (𝅗𝅥 + 𝅗𝅥.) + o x = (𝅗𝅥. * 𝅗𝅥.)

30. o x + (o + 𝅗𝅥) = 10

31. (𝅗𝅥. + 𝅗𝅥.) + (𝅗𝅥. + 𝅗𝅥)x + x = 𝅗𝅥. * 𝅗𝅥

32. o + 𝅗𝅥. x + 𝅗𝅥 x = 9

33. (𝅗𝅥. * 𝅗𝅥)x + 𝅗𝅥. + 𝅗𝅥. x = 21

34. 𝅗𝅥 x + 𝅗𝅥 = x + 𝅗𝅥

35. 7(𝅗𝅥. x + 𝅗𝅥) = 266

36. x + 𝅗𝅥. y = o * 𝅗𝅥

    -x + (𝅗𝅥. + 𝅗𝅥)y = 0

37. 𝅗𝅥 x + o y = o * 𝅗𝅥.

    𝅗𝅥 x + 𝅗𝅥. y = 17

38. -𝅗𝅥. + x = ▬

39. 11 = 9 + x

40. 𝅗𝅥. = 𝅗𝅥. **Z**

41. 13x + 6 = 201

42. 𝅗𝅥. * 𝅗𝅥. = 7**Z** + ♩

43. 19 = x + ♩

44. 11 = 5x + 11

45. y – 𝅗𝅥. = (♩ + ♪)

46. 54 = ♩ + ♩**Z** + ♩**Z**

47. z – (𝅗𝅥. * ♩) = ♫

48. k – (𝅝 * ♩ + 𝄾) = 𝅝

49. m – ♫ = (♩ + ♩ * 𝅗𝅥.)

50. g – 𝅝 = (𝄼 + ♬)

51. t – (𝅝 * ♩) = 0

52. $x - (o + 𝅗𝅥.) = 𝅗𝅥.$

53. $o\, y + 𝅗𝅥. = 7y - 21$

54. $𝅗𝅥 (𝅗𝅥. * 𝅗𝅥\, z + 15) = 198$

55. $x - ♫ = -𝄾♪$

56. $z - (o * 𝅗𝅥 + 𝅗𝅥) = -𝅗𝅥$

57. $k - (♩ - 𝅗𝅥) = -(𝅗𝅥 + 𝅗𝅥)$

58. $n - (o + ♩) = -𝅗𝅥.$

59. $r - (𝅗𝅥. * 𝅗𝅥) = -9$

60. $s - (o * 𝅗𝅥) = -7$

61. $x - 32 = 11$

62. $y - 𝅗𝅥 = -(o * 𝅗𝅥)$

63. $y - 25 = o$

64. $h - 9 = -20$

65. $m - 13 = 15$

66. $\text{♩} - 21 = -18$

67. $n - 25 = -30$

68. $s - 8 = 14$

69. $7 = s - 9$

70. $-10 = k - 11$

71. $-12 = w - 8$

72. $21 = r - 12$

73. $19 = u - 5$

74. $-16 = p - 25$

75. $-31 = q - 8$

76. $10 = v - 14$

77. $5m = 10$

78. 𝅗𝅥 k = 𝅗𝅥. * 𝅗𝅥

79. 𝅗𝅥. t = 9

80. 𝅝 h = 𝅝 * 𝅝

81. ____ ÷ 7 = 𝅝

82. z − ♩ + 𝅝 =

83. $c^2 + c + c =$

84. 𝅗𝅥. x = (♫ − ♩)

85. −𝅗𝅥 y^2 = y^2 + 5

86. x + x − ♩ =

87. m + ♩ = (𝅗𝅥. * 𝅗𝅥)

   ♩ + n + m = (𝅝 * 𝅗𝅥.)

88. r + ♩ = 𝅝 + 𝅝 + 𝅗𝅥

89. −𝅗𝅥 k = −(𝄼 * 𝄼)

90. 𝅝 w = −𝅝

91. r + half = o + half + o

92. s + quarter + r = 19

93. $\left(\text{dotted half} * \text{half}\right)$ + p = 13

94. q + p + 6 = 19

95. $\text{dotted half} \cdot x$ + four sixteenths = -1/3

96. $\text{dotted eighth} + \text{sixteenth}$ + half - x = half

97. quarter + eighth triplet + dotted half - x = dotted half

98. dotted half + eighth * o - x = o

99. four sixteenths + eighth group + eighth group * four eighths - rest = half

100. $\quad$ dotted half - $\text{dotted eighth + sixteenth}$ + eighth - x = 0

COMBINATION

1. ♩² + ♪ + ♩. + ♫ ÷ √𝅝 =

2. (♩ + ♩) + (𝅗𝅥 + ♩) − (𝅗𝅥 − 𝅝) =

3. 𝅝 + ♩. − ♩ * 𝅗𝅥 + ♫ ♫♫ ÷ 𝅗𝅥 =

4. 𝅗𝅥 * ♩ + ♩. − ♩ * 𝅝 − ♪ =

5. ♫♫ + 𝅝 − 𝅗𝅥 * ♩. + ♩ ÷ 𝅗𝅥 =

6. ♩. * 𝅘𝅥𝅯𝅘𝅥𝅯 𝅘𝅥𝅯𝅘𝅥𝅯 + 𝅝 − 𝅗𝅥 ÷ ♫♫ =

7. ♩ − 𝄾 + ♫ + 𝄼 * 𝅗𝅥 ÷ 𝄺 + 𝄾 =

8. 𝅝 + ♩. − 𝄾 + ♫♫ * 𝅗𝅥 ÷ 𝅗𝅥 * √(♩. * ♩.) =

9. ♩² * ♩ + ♩. − ♩ * 𝅝 − ♪ =

10. 𝅝² ÷ (♫♫ + ♩) + ♩. * 𝅗𝅥 − ♪ =

11. 7 * ____ = 42

12. 8 * ____ = 48

13. (𝅘𝅥𝅯𝅘𝅥𝅯𝅘𝅥𝅯𝅘𝅥𝅯 + 𝅗𝅥) − 𝅘𝅥𝅮𝅘𝅥𝅮𝅘𝅥𝅮 =

14. 𝅘𝅥𝅮𝅘𝅥𝅮𝅘𝅥 + 𝅘𝅥𝅮𝅘𝅥𝅮𝅘𝅥(3) + 𝅘𝅥𝅮 − 𝅘𝅥𝅮 =

15. 𝅘𝅥𝅮 + 𝄾 − 𝄾 =

16. 𝅗𝅥. + 𝅘𝅥𝅮 * 𝅗𝅥. =

17. 𝅝 * 𝅝 * 𝅗𝅥 =

18. (𝄻 + 𝄼) − (𝅘𝅥.𝅘𝅥𝅮 + 𝅘𝅥𝅮𝅘𝅥.) =

19. x − 𝅘𝅥𝅘𝅥 = _ 𝄾𝅘𝅥𝅮

20. ___ ÷ (𝅝 * 𝅗𝅥 * 𝅘𝅥) = 𝅗𝅥

21. 𝅝 * 𝅗𝅥. =

22. (𝅝 + 𝅗𝅥. + 𝄼) * 𝅘𝅥 =

23. (𝅗𝅥. + 𝅗𝅥 + 𝄾 + 𝅘𝅥) * 𝅗𝅥. =

24. 𝄾 * 𝅘𝅥𝅘𝅥 =

25. 𝅝 − 𝅘𝅥𝅮 − 𝄾 − 𝅘𝅥𝅮 − 𝄾 =

26. 𝄾 − 𝄾 =

27. 𝅗𝅥· − 𝅗𝅥 =

28. (𝅗𝅥· * 𝅗𝅥·) − (𝅗𝅥 + 𝄾) − 𝄾 − 𝅘𝅥𝅮 =

29. _____ ÷ (𝅗𝅥· * 𝅗𝅥) = (𝅗𝅥 * 𝅗𝅥· * 𝄼)

30. 𝅗𝅥 + 𝅝 ² =

31. 𝅘𝅥𝅮𝅘𝅥𝅮𝅘𝅥𝅮 + 𝅝 − 𝅗𝅥 * 𝅗𝅥· + 𝅘𝅥 ÷ 𝅗𝅥 =

32. 𝅝 + 𝅗𝅥· =

33. 𝅗𝅥 + 𝅗𝅥 + 𝅗𝅥· + 𝅘𝅥𝅮𝅘𝅥𝅮 + 𝅘𝅥 + 𝅗𝅥 =

34. 𝅗𝅥· + 𝅗𝅥· + 𝅝 + 𝅗𝅥· =

35. 𝅝 + 𝅘𝅥 + 𝅗𝅥· + 𝅘𝅥𝅮𝅘𝅥𝅮 + 𝅗𝅥 =

36. (𝅝 + 𝅗𝅥· + 𝅗𝅥) + (𝅗𝅥 + 𝅘𝅥𝅮𝅘𝅥𝅮 + 𝅘𝅥𝅮𝅘𝅥𝅮𝅘𝅥𝅮) =

37. (𝅘𝅥𝅮𝅘𝅥𝅮 + 𝅘𝅥) + (𝅝 + 𝅗𝅥· + 𝅗𝅥) =

38. (𝅗𝅥 + 𝅗𝅥) + 𝅘𝅥𝅮𝅘𝅥𝅮𝅘𝅥𝅮𝅘𝅥𝅮 =

39. ♩ + ♩ =

40. ♩ + (𝅝 + ♩. + ♩) =

41. ♩ − ♫♫ =

42. (♩. + ♪) − (𝄽 + 𝄾) =

43. (▬ + 𝄾) − (♩. + 𝄾) =

44. ♩. − (♩ + ♪) =

45. (𝄽 + ♪) − ♪ =

46. (♩. + 𝄾) − (♩ + ♪) =

47. (𝅝 + ♪) − ♫♫♪ =

48. (♩. * ♩.) − (𝅝 + ♪) =

49. 𝅝 ² − (♩ ² + ♪) =

50. (▬ * ♩.) − (♩. * ♩. + 𝄾) =

51. (𝅝 + ♩ + ♪) − (♩. + ♪) =

52. $\left(\text{𝅗𝅥.} + \text{𝄾} \right) - \text{♪} =$

53. $\left(\text{𝅗𝅥.} * \text{♫.} \right) - \text{𝅗𝅥} - \text{♪} =$

54. $\text{𝅝} - \text{♪} - \text{𝄾} - \text{♪} - \text{𝄾} =$

55. $\text{𝄾} - \text{𝄾} =$

56. $\text{𝅗𝅥.} - \text{𝅗𝅥} =$

57. $\left(\text{𝅝} * \text{𝅗𝅥} + \text{𝅗𝅥.} \right) =$

58. $\text{𝅗𝅥} - \left(\text{𝅗𝅥} - \text{𝅗𝅥} \right) =$

59. $\text{𝅗𝅥} + \text{♩} =$

60. $\text{𝅝} + \text{𝅗𝅥} =$

61. $\text{𝅝} + \text{𝅝} + \text{♫} + \left(\text{𝅝} * \text{𝅗𝅥} \right) =$

62. $\text{𝅝} + \text{𝅗𝅥} + \text{𝅗𝅥} =$

63. $\text{𝅗𝅥} + \text{𝄾} =$

64. $\text{♫} - \text{𝅗𝅥} - \text{𝅗𝅥} =$

65. ♪ + ♩. + 𝅝 =

66. ♩. ♪ + ♪ =

67. ♫ + ♪♫ + ♬♬ =

68. (♫ + ♪♪) – ♪ =

69. 𝄾 + ♩. + ♩ =

70. ♩ – ♩ + ♪ =

71. 𝄽 + ♩. + ♩. + ♩. =

72. 𝄾 + ♪ – ♪ =

73. ♪ + ♪ =

74. ♩. – ♪ =

75. ♪ + ♩ – 𝄾 =

76. ♩ + ▬ + 𝄾 =

77. ♩ – 𝄾 =

78. 𝅗𝅥 ＊ 𝄽 ＋ 𝅝 =

79. 𝅗𝅥. ＋ 𝅗𝅥 ＋ ♪ =

80. 𝅗𝅥 ＋ 𝅗𝅥. ＋ 𝅗𝅥 =

81. ♫ ＊ ♪♪ =

82. 𝅝 ＊ 𝅗𝅥. =

83. ＿＿ ÷ (𝅝 ＋ 𝅗𝅥.) = (𝅝 ＊ 𝅗𝅥)

84. (𝅗𝅥 ＋ 𝅗𝅥.) ＊ (𝅝 ＋ 𝅝) =

85. ＿＿ ÷ (♫ ＋ 𝅝) ＊ 𝅗𝅥 − 𝅘𝅥 = 𝅗𝅥. ＋ 𝅝

86. 𝅗𝅥 ＊ 𝅗𝅥. ＋ 𝅝 =

87. 𝅗𝅥 ÷ 𝅗𝅥 =

88. ＿＿ ÷ (𝅗𝅥. ＊ 𝅗𝅥.) = 𝅗𝅥.

89. ＿＿ ÷ (𝅝 ＋ 𝅗𝅥.) = (𝅗𝅥. ＊ 𝅗𝅥)

90. (♫ ＋ 𝅗𝅥 ＋ 𝅗𝅥.) ＊ (♫ ＋ 𝄽 ＋ 𝅘𝅥 ＋ 𝅗𝅥.) =

91. 𝅗𝅥. * 𝅗𝅥. * 𝅗𝅥. =

92. (𝄾♪ * 𝅗𝅥) + 𝄽 + ♩ =

93. (𝅗𝅥. + 𝅗𝅥) * (𝅗𝅥. + 𝅗𝅥) =

94. o * 𝅗𝅥. * o * 𝅗𝅥. =

95. o x = 𝅗𝅥. − ♫

96. x − o + 𝅗𝅥. x =

97. (𝅗𝅥. * ♩) − o − ♪ =

98. ♩ − 𝄾 + ♪♪ * 𝅗𝅥 =

99. o + 𝅗𝅥. − 𝄽 * 𝅗𝅥 =

100.   x − ♫ = 𝅗𝅥.

NOTATION KEY

Whole note	o	**4 counts**
Whole rest	▬	**4 counts**
Dotted half note	♩.	**3 counts**
Half note	♩	**2 counts**
Half rest	▬	**2 counts**
Quarter note	♩	**1 count**
Quarter rest	𝄽	**1 count**
Eighth note	♪	**½ count**
Eighth rest	𝄾	**½ count**
Sixteeth note	♬	**¼ count**
Sixteeth rest	𝄿	**¼ count**

Nydia Kelly is the owner of Gwinnett Academy of Music in Snellville, Georgia. Over the years of teaching, she realized that a large number of her students were having problems manipulating musical note values to count their music. She decided to create simple mathematical equations using musical notation and it has quickly become a popular part of lessons for her students.